by Iain Gray

WRITING *to* REMEMBER

79 Main Street, Newtongrange,
Midlothian EH22 4NA
Tel: 0131 344 0414   Fax: 0845 075 6085
E-mail: info@lang-syne.co.uk
www.langsyneshop.co.uk

Design by Dorothy Meikle
Printed by Printwell Ltd
© Lang Syne Publishers Ltd 2020

All rights reserved. No part of this publication may be reproduced, stored or introduced into a retrieval system, or transmitted in any form or by any means (electronic, mechanical, photocopying, recording or otherwise) without the prior written permission of Lang Syne Publishers Ltd.

ISBN 978-1-85217-379-1

White

MOTTOES include:
Royal is my Race
(MacGregor)
and
Acquired by Work

CREST:
A Gold Lion's Head
wearing an antique Crown

NAME variations include:
Whyte
Wight

The spirit of the clan means much to thousands of people

Chapter one:

The origins of the clan system

by Rennie McOwan

The original Scottish clans of the Highlands and the great families of the Lowlands and Borders were gatherings of families, relatives, allies and neighbours for mutual protection against rivals or invaders.

Scotland experienced invasion from the Vikings, the Romans and English armies from the south. The Norman invasion of what is now England also had an influence on land-holding in Scotland. Some of these invaders stayed on and in time became 'Scottish'.

The word clan derives from the Gaelic language term 'clann', meaning children, and it was first used many centuries ago as communities were formed around tribal lands in glens and mountain fastnesses.

The format of clans changed over the centuries, but at its best the chief and his family held the land on behalf of all, like trustees, and the ordinary clansmen and women believed they had a blood relationship with the founder of their clan.

There were two way duties and obligations. An inadequate chief could be deposed and replaced by someone of greater ability.

Clan people had an immense pride in race. Their relationship with the chief was like adult children to a father and they had a real dignity.

The concept of clanship is very old and a more feudal notion of authority gradually crept in.

Pictland, for instance, was divided into seven principalities ruled by feudal leaders who were the strongest and most charismatic leaders of their particular groups.

By the sixth century the 'British' kingdoms of Strathclyde, Lothian and Celtic Dalriada (Argyll) had emerged and Scotland, as one nation, began to take shape in the time of King Kenneth MacAlpin.

Some chiefs claimed descent from ancient kings which may not have been accurate in every case.

By the twelfth and thirteenth centuries the clans and families were more strongly brought under the central control of Scottish monarchs.

Lands were awarded and administered more and more under royal favour, yet the power of the area clan chiefs was still very great.

The long wars to ensure Scotland's

independence against the expansionist ideas of English monarchs extended the influence of some clans and reduced the lands of others.

Those who supported Scotland's greatest king, Robert the Bruce, were awarded the territories of the families who had opposed his claim to the Scottish throne.

In the Scottish Borders country – the notorious Debatable Lands – the great families built up a ferocious reputation for providing warlike men accustomed to raiding into England and occasionally fighting one another.

Chiefs had the power to dispense justice and to confiscate lands and clan warfare produced a society where martial virtues – courage, hardiness, tenacity – were greatly admired.

Gradually the relationship between the clans and the Crown became strained as Scottish monarchs became more orientated to life in the Lowlands and, on occasion, towards England.

The Highland clans spoke a different language, Gaelic, whereas the language of Lowland Scotland and the court was Scots and in more modern times, English.

Highlanders dressed differently, had different

customs, and their wild mountain land sometimes seemed almost foreign to people living in the Lowlands.

It must be emphasised that Gaelic culture was very rich and story-telling, poetry, piping, the clarsach (harp) and other music all flourished and were greatly respected.

Highland culture was different from other parts of Scotland but it was not inferior or less sophisticated.

Central Government, whether in London or Edinburgh, sometimes saw the Gaelic clans as a challenge to their authority and some sent expeditions into the Highlands and west to crush the power of the Lords of the Isles.

Nevertheless, when the eighteenth century Jacobite Risings came along the cause of the Stuarts was mainly supported by Highland clans.

The word Jacobite comes from the Latin for James – Jacobus. The Jacobites wanted to restore the exiled Stuarts to the throne of Britain.

The monarchies of Scotland and England became one in 1603 when King James VI of Scotland (1st of England) gained the English throne after Queen Elizabeth died.

The Union of Parliaments of Scotland and England, the Treaty of Union, took place in 1707.

Some Highland clans, of course, and Lowland families opposed the Jacobites and supported the incoming Hanoverians.

After the Jacobite cause finally went down at Culloden in 1746 a kind of ethnic cleansing took place. The power of the chiefs was curtailed. Tartan and the pipes were banned in law.

Many emigrated, some because they wanted to, some because they were evicted by force. In addition, many Highlanders left for the cities of the south to seek work.

Many of the clan lands became home to sheep and deer shooting estates.

But the warlike traditions of the clans and the great Lowland and Border families lived on, with their descendants fighting bravely for freedom in two world wars.

Remember the men from whence you came, says the Gaelic proverb, and to that could be added the role of many heroic women.

The spirit of the clan, of having roots, whether Highland or Lowland, means much to thousands of people.

Meanwhile, many families proudly boast the heraldic device known as a Coat of Arms, as featured on our front cover.

The central motif of the Coat of Arms would originally have been what was sometimes borne on the shield of a warrior to distinguish himself from others on the battlefield.

Not featured on the Coat of Arms, but highlighted on page three, is the family motto and related crest – with the latter frequently different from the central motif.

Clan warfare produced a society where courage and tenacity were greatly admired

Chapter two:

Kinship with the clans

There is much more colour to the name of White than it may first suggest as, peeling back the layers of history and also looking to the present day, it is revealed how bearers of the name have achieved fame and distinction.

Derived from the Old English 'hwit', indicating 'white', it came to variously refer to someone with fair hair, fair complexion, or even someone who wore white clothing.

Found from earliest times in various forms that include 'Huita', 'Huuita', 'Hwite', 'Quhyt', 'Quhit' and 'Whyte', it is recorded in Scotland in the early fourteenth century – with an Adam Quhyt in receipt of a charter of land at Barskimming, in northern Ayrshire, at the time of the great warrior king Robert the Bruce.

An Andrew Quhit is recorded in the royal burgh of Brechin, in Angus, in 1472, while in 1658 Robert Whyte is recorded as being provost of Kirkcaldy, in Fife.

The Gaelic form of the name is

'MacGhillebhain', and it may well have been under this form that the ancestors of the Whites of today forged a close kinship with the proud Scottish clans of Lamont and MacGregor.

This kinship was so close that the Whites are regarded as septs, or sub-branches, of these clans and accordingly entitled to share in their heritage and traditions.

But there are tragic and bloody reasons why the Whites and their namesakes the Whytes came to be regarded as septs of these clans.

'Neither spare nor dispose' is the motto, and a raised right hand with the palm facing outwards is the crest of the Lamonts – who boast an ancient Celtic pedigree that can be traced back to a branch of the famed royal house of the O'Neils of Ulster.

From well before the twelfth century, they were inpossession of the bulk of the territory of Cowal, in Argyll, but in later centuries it was their fatal misfortune to incur the enmity of the avaricious and equally proud clan of the Campbells of Argyll.

This came to a head in June of 1646 when the Campbells laid siege to the Lamont stronghold of Castle Toward, south of Inellan, and the clan Chief Sir James Lamont was forced into surrender – but only after he received an assurance that his kinsfolk would not be molested and the Lamont estates spared from plunder and destruction.

No sooner had the surrender terms been agreed than Sir James and some of his closest relatives, including his brother, were taken into captivity, while about 200 of his kinsfolk were rounded up, thrown into boats, and taken north to Dunoon.

Arriving at a hill known as Tom-a-Mhoid, which, ironically, is the Gaelic rendering for 'Hill of Justice', nearly forty men described as 'leading gentlemen' of the Lamonts, were hanged from an ash tree that grew behind a nearby churchyard.

Taken down while still alive, they were cast into hastily dug pits, while the rest of the prisoners, including women and children and the elderly, were stabbed and bludgeoned and also thrown into the pits.

The frenzied orgies of bloodlust over, the pits were covered with earth, leaving those still alive to slowly suffocate to death.

The Lamont lands on Cowal were ravaged, and a number of clanswomen who had escaped the original deportation to Dunoon were hunted down and killed, and their bodies left 'for a prey to ravenous beasts and fowls.'

The Lamont strongholds of Toward and Ascog were burned to the ground and Sir James imprisoned for a time at Inveraray.

Imprisoned later at Dunstaffnage, he was forced to sign a document surrendering all his estates.

In the interim, surviving Lamonts were either driven from their ancestral lands or forced to assume new identities by taking on new surnames – including White, Brown and Black.

This is why any Whites of today who can trace a descent back to Cowal, in Argyll, could well be descendants of these original Lamonts.

'S'rioghal mo dhream' ('Royal is my race') is the motto, and a lion's head crowned with an antique crown is the crest of the MacGregors – a clan that claims an ancient descent from Griogar, or Gregor, a son of Alpin, who was a king of Dalriada.

With their proud name proscribed, or banned, in later centuries, many were forced to assume new identities by adopting new names such as White.

These aliases were among a host of others adopted by the clan, and the official Clan Gregor Society, founded in 1822 and one of the oldest clan societies, stresses that only Whites who can trace a connection back to the ancient MacGregor homelands may be entitled to share in the clan's heritage and traditions.

The western borders of Perthshire and the eastern borders of Argyll had been from time immemorial the homelands of the clan – lands that included Glengyle, Glenlyon and Glenstrae.

But Clan Campbell steadily encroached on these lands, until the MacGregors found themselves in the humiliating role of mere tenants on what had for centuries been their own lands.

Rebelling against this, they found an outlet for their passions by preying on their rather more law-abiding neighbours.

On two occasions during the reign of Mary, Queen of Scots, what were known as commissions of fire and sword were issued to clan chiefs who were victims of MacGregor raiding and pillaging.

This gave them virtual carte blanche to kill any MacGregor on sight and impound or destroy their property.

An Act of Council, imposing further severe sanctions on the unruly clan, was passed in 1603, and the very name of MacGregor was banned.

A commission was granted eight years later to 'root out and extirpate' the MacGregors, while they were also forbidden to carry any weapons, apart from a pointless knife to cut their meat, and no more than four were allowed to gather together at any one time.

These harsh measures were re-enacted in 1617 and 1635, rescinded for a time on the Restoration to the throne of Charles II in 1660, but restored again in 1693.

It was not until 1774 that the proscription on the name MacGregor was at last lifted and, while many who had been forced to adopt new names reverted back to MacGregor, others who had chosen aliases such as White retained this new name.

Chapter three:

Honours and fame

Across the Atlantic, Whites quite literally gained an early foothold on the shores of North America.

This was through Peregrine White, the first English child born to the Pilgrims in the New World.

His mother gave birth to him shortly before the Pilgrim's ship, *Mayflower*, docked at Provincetown Harbor, in Provincetown, Massachusetts, in November 1620, and he was named Peregrine because the name denotes 'one who journeys to foreign lands', or 'pilgrim'.

Not much is known of his later life, although he is understood to have held a number of civil and military posts before his death in Massachusetts in 1703.

There is a record, however, of him and his future wife Susan being fined by the Puritanical authorities 'for fornication before marriage or contract.'

The couple later married and went on to have seven children.

Another early New World pioneer of the

name of White was James White, born in 1747 in Rowan County, North Carolina.

Serving as a captain in the North Carolina militia during the American Revolutionary War of 1775 to 1783, it was he who founded White's Fort, later Knoxville, Tennessee, before his death in 1821.

Another American 'founder' was Andrew Dickson White, the diplomat and historian who was born in Homer, New York City, in 1832 and who died in 1918.

The son of a wealthy banker, it was he who, along with the entrepreneur Ezra Cornell, co-founded the centre of academic excellence known today as Cornell University, serving as its first president from 1866 to 1885.

In more contemporary times, a pioneer of a different sort, this time of space exploration, was Lieutenant Colonel Edward White, better known as Ed White, the U.S. Air Force officer and NASA astronaut who, on June 3, 1965, became the first American to conduct a space walk.

Born in 1930 in San Antonio, Texas, he was among three astronauts killed in January of 1967 in a fire that broke out during a training exercise at the Kennedy Space Center at Cape Canaveral.

Bearers of the White name have also gained distinction on the battlefield.

Born Jacob Weiss in Leeds, Yorkshire, in 1896, the son of Jewish immigrants from Russia, Jack White was a First World War recipient of the Victoria Cross (VC), the highest award for bravery in the face of enemy action for British and Commonwealth forces.

He had been a private with the 6th King's Own Royal Regiment (Lancaster), when, in action in March 1917 at the Dialah River, Mesopotamia, he used a pontoon to ferry wounded comrades to safety across the river.

Later promoted to Lance Corporal, he was refused permission to enlist in Britain's Home Guard during the Second World War, because the nit-picking and small-minded authorities claimed his parents had failed to be properly naturalised as British citizens – this despite the fact that he had been born in Yorkshire and was a holder of the VC.

Field Marshall Sir George White, born in 1835 at Port Stewart, Co. Londonderry, and who died in 1912, was an Irish recipient of the VC.

He had been second in command of the 92nd Regiment (later the Gordon Highlanders) during the Second Anglo-Afghan War when, in October of 1879, he led a successful personal assault, armed only with a rifle, on a fortified hill.

He shot the enemy leader, while the rest panicked and fled.

Later appointed Commander-in-Chief, India, he died in 1912, while his son, Jack White, was the Irish Republican who in 1913 co-founded the Irish Citizen Army along with James Connolly.

In politics, James Whyte was the Scots-Australian politician who was born in 1820 near Greenlaw, Berwickshire, in the Scottish Borders, and who died in 1882.

Immigrating in 1832 to what was then Van Dieman's Land, now Tasmania, he served as 6th Premier of Tasmania from 1863 to 1866.

In the realms of political activism, Walter White, born in 1893 in Atlanta, Georgia, was the distinguished African American who served as executive secretary from 1931 until his death in 1955 of the National Association for the Advancement of Coloured People.

In Canada, William Andrew White III, better known as Bill White, was the composer and activist for social justice who was born in 1915 in Truro, Nova Scotia.

In 1949 he became the first black Canadian to run for federal office, as the Co-operative and Commonwealth Federation candidate for the Spadina constituency.

He was appointed an Officer of the Order of Canada eleven years before his death in 1981, for services to the community and his contribution to better relations and understanding between peoples of different racial background.

It is perhaps apt that, bearing in mind their own historical roles, bearers of the White name have also been noted recorders of some of the most momentous events in history.

Born in 1904 in the Bronx district of New York, Margaret Bourke-White was the renowned American photographer who had a special gift of being in the right place at the right time.

Appointed associate editor of *Fortune* magazine in 1929, a year later she became the first Western photographer allowed into the Soviet Union, and was later hired as *Life* magazine's first female staff photographer.

She recorded stark images of drought victims of America's Dust Bowl during the mid-1930s, while during the Second World War she became the first female war correspondent and the first woman allowed into combat zones.

Known as "Maggie the Indestructible" by her *Life* magazine colleagues, she survived many dangerous encounters, and at the close of the war had the grim task of photographing the horror of the newly liberated Buchenwald concentration camp.

Her camera was also to hand in 1948 when the great Indian patriot, moral teacher and social reformer Mahatma Gandhi was assassinated while en route to a prayer meeting.

Her autobiographical *Portrait of Myself* was published eight years before her death in 1971, and she was portrayed by the actress Candice Bergen in the 1982 film *Gandhi* and by Farrah Fawcett in the television film *Double Exposure: The Story of Margaret Bourke-White*.

Also behind the camera lens, John H. White, born in 1945 in Lexington, North Carolina, is the *Chicago Sun Times* photojournalist who was awarded a Pulitzer Prize in 1982 for his 'consistently excellent work on a variety of subjects.'

A recorder of historical events through the medium of the pen, rather than the camera, Theodore White, born in Boston in 1915, was one of the twentieth century's leading American political historians and journalists.

He was *Time* magazine's correspondent in China during the Second World War, his experiences there subsequently documented in his 1946 *Thunder Out of China*, but he is best known for his detailed accounts and analysis of the 1960, 1964, 1968 and 1972 U.S. presidential elections.

These were published as best-selling books, one of which, *The Making of the President*, 1960, won a Pulitzer Prize for general non-fiction.

His *Breach of Faith: The Fall of Richard Nixon*, was published eleven years before his death in 1986.

Chapter four:

On the world stage

Bearers of the White and Whyte names have also achieved fame through a colourful range of other pursuits.

The recipient of a 2010 Screen Actors Guild Lifetime Achievement Award, **Betty White** is the veteran American actress and comedian who was born in 1922 in Oak Park, Illinois.

Her best known roles include that of Sue Ann Nivens on *The Mary Tyler Moore* television show – for which she won a 1975 Emmy Award for Outstanding Support Actress in a Comedy Show – and that of Rose Nyland in *The Golden Girls*, for which she received the 1986 Emmy Award for Outstanding Lead Actress.

Born in 1904 in Paterson, New Jersey, **Alva White** was the American actress who starred in films that include the 1928 *Show Girl* and, from 1949, *Flamingo Road*.

The actress, who died in 1983, has a star on the Hollywood Walk of Fame.

Best known for her role in the British

television drama *Life on Mars*, **Liz White** is the actress who was born in 1979 in Rotherham, South Yorkshire, while **Karen White**, born in Philadelphia in 1965, is the American film and television actress who first came to fame in the role from 1990 to 1992 of Charmiane Brown in the television sitcom *The Cosby Show*.

Born in 1950 in London, **Shiela White** is the English actress of stage and television series that include the 1976 *I, Claudius*, while **Larry Grayson** was the stage name of the English stand-up comedian and television presenter William Sulley White, who was born in 1923 in Banbury, Oxfordshire.

The host of such popular series as *The Generation Game* and the 1975 show *Shut that Door!* – his catchphrase – he died in 1995.

From the stage to music, no less than three bearers of the White name are renowned drummers.

Born in 1930 in Glasgow, **Andy White** is the Scottish drummer who has the rare distinction as having played on one of the Beatles' hits.

This was in September of 1962 when record producer George Martin was dissatisfied with Ringo Starr's drumming on the band's first single, *Love Me Do*, and drafted in session musician White to replace him for the recording and for the B-side, *P.S. I Love You*.

The single went on to become a major international hit – but White is reported to have received only £57 for the session and does not share in any of the massive royalties that have accrued over the years.

Born in 1972 in Eltham, London, **Alan White** is the drummer best known for having played with the British rock group Oasis between 1995 and 2004.

Yet another **Alan White**, born in 1949 in Pelton, County Durham, is the drummer who, in addition to having performed with the progressive rock group Yes, also played for John Lennon's plastic Ono Band and on Lennon's *Imagine* album.

Behind the microphone, **Barry White** – born Barrenco Eugene Carter in Galveston, Texas, in 1944 – was the multi-award winning singer, songwriter, arranger and record producer who's many major hits include the 1973 *I'm Gonna Love You Just a Little Bit More, Baby* and the 1978 *Your Sweetness is My Weakness*.

He died in 2003, while to date his record sales exceed 100 million.

In contemporary rock music, **Snowy White**, born Terence White in 1948 in Devon, is the guitarist who played with Thin Lizzy from 1979 to 1981 and whose solo single, *Bird Of Paradise*, was a UK Top Ten hit in 1983.

Back across the Atlantic, Booker T. Washington White, born in Mississippi in 1906 and who died in 1977, was the blues guitarist and singer better known as **Bukka White**.

A cousin of the legendary blues guitarist B.B. King, he was inducted into the Blues Hall of Fame in 1990.

In Scotland, **Tam White** is the musician and actor, born in Edinburgh in 1942, who provided the vocals for the actor Robbie Coltrane to mime his character of Big Jazza McGlone in the 1987 British television series *Tutti Frutti*.

In Scottish folk music, **Alasdair White**, born in 1983 on Lewis, in the Outer Hebrides, has been the fiddle player since 2001 with the Battlefield Band. He also enjoys a successful solo career.

An inductee of the Rock and Roll Hall of Fame and the Vocal Group Hall of Fame through his membership of the American band Earth, Wind and Fire, **Maurice White** is the singer, songwriter, arranger and record producer who was born in 1941 in Memphis, Tennessee.

Founded by White in the early 1970s, Earth, Wind and Fire, one of whose most famous hits is the 1976 *Got to Get You into My Life*, have to date sold more than 90 million albums worldwide.

From music to the highly competitive world of sport, **Jimmy White** is the English snooker player who was born in 1962 in the Tooting district of London.

Nicknamed "The Whirlwind", he began his professional career in 1980 after winning that year's Amateur World Championship, and went on to compete in the finals of six professional world championships.

Although he did not win any of these, he was at one time ranked No. 2 in the world, while in 1984 he shared the World Doubles Championship with Alex "Hurricane" Higgins.

In baseball, **Bill White** is the former first baseman who was born in 1934 in Lakewood, Florida.

Teams he played for include the New York Giants and the San Francisco Giants and, from 1966 to 1968, the Philadelphia Phillies, while from 1989 to 1994 he was president of the sport's National League – the first African American to hold the post.

On the ice, **Charlie White**, born in 1987 in Dearborn, Michigan is the American ice dancer who, along with partner Meryl Davis, won the 2009 and 2010 U.S. National Championships and a silver medal at the 2010 Winter Olympics in Vancouver.

In ice hockey, **John White**, born in 1977 in New Glasgow, Nova Scotia, is the Canadian defenceman who was a member of the New Jersey Devils team of the National Hockey League that won the Stanley Cup in 2000 and 2003.

Nicknamed "The Flying Tomato" because of his shock of red hair, **Shaun White**, born in 1986 in San Diego, is the American snowboarder who won gold in the 'halfpipe' events at the both the 2006 and 2010 Winter Olympics.

On the rugby pitch, **Des White** is the former rugby league fullback recognised as having been one of New Zealand's greatest players of the game.

Born in 1927, he is remembered for having kicked a world record of eleven goals, against Australia, in 1952.

In Scotland, **Derek Whyte**, born in Glasgow in 1968, is the former player with teams that include Celtic, Aberdeen and Middlesbrough and who was a member of the national team from 1987 to 1999.

In American football, **Reggie White**, born in 1961 in Chattanooga, Tennessee, was the American defensive end who played for 15 seasons from 1984 for teams that include the Philadelphia Eagles, Green Bay Packers and Carolina Panthers.

Bearers of the White and Whyte names have also gained distinction in the creative world of literature.

Recognised as one of the greatest English language writers of the twentieth century, **Patrick White** was the British-born Australian novelist who, from 1935 until his death in 1990, produced twelve novels, two collections of novels and eight plays.

Born in 1912 in Knightsbridge, London but later moving to Sydney with his family when aged only six months, in 1973 he became the first Australian to receive the Nobel Prize for Literature – 'for an epic and psychological narrative art, which has introduced a new continent into literature.'

White, whose acclaimed novels include the 1939 *Happy Valley*, the 1957 *Voss* and the 1966 *The Solid Mandala*, used the money from his Nobel Prize to establish a trust to fund Australia's annual Patrick White Award for creative writers.

Born in India in 1906 of English parentage, Terence Hanbury White, better known as **T.H. White**, was the writer best remembered for his *The Once and Future King* series of Arthurian novels, including the 1938 *The Sword in the Stone* and the 1946 *The Candle in the Wind*.

It was after his death in 1964 that the series inspired the Broadway musical *Camelot* and the Disney animated film *The Sword in the Stone*.

A member of the American Academy of Arts and Letters, **Edmund White III.**, born in 1944 in Cincinnati, is the acclaimed American author and literary critic whose novels include the 1973 *Forgetting Elena*, while **Jack Whyte**, born in 1940, is the Scots-Canadian novelist whose work includes the Knights Templar trilogy of *Knights of the Black and White*, *Standard of Honour* and the 2009 *Order in Chaos*.

In the realms of science fiction, **James White**, born in Belfast in 1928, was the Northern Irish novelist whose books include the 1962 *Hospital Station*, the 1991 *The Silent Stars Go By* and, published in the year of his death in 1999, *Earth: Final Conflict*.

Best known for her 1936 novel *The Wheel Spins*, later memorably adapted for film by Alfred Hitchcock as *The Lady Vanishes*, **Ethel White** was the Welsh crime writer born in 1876 in Abergavenny and who died in 1944.

Winner of an honorary Pulitzer Prize in 1978, Elwyn Brooks White, better known as **E.B. White**, was the American author of both children's and adult books who was born in 1899 in Mt. Vernon, New York.

White, who died in 1985, was the author of books that include his 1945 *Stuart Little*, later adapted as an animated film of the same name.

Every family has the odd skeleton or two rattling around in the closet, and no less so than the international family of Whites.

This is in the form of William Jack White, better known as the feared gangster of the American Prohibition era **Three Fingers White**.

Born in 1900, his nickname stemmed from a childhood accident in which he lost two fingers from his right hand – but unfortunately for his gangland rivals these did not include his rather itchy trigger finger.

Declared a public enemy in the Chicago Crime Commission report of 1923 as a member of the notorious Johnny Turrio-Al Capone crime syndicate, he was shot to death eleven years later by rival gunmen.